Snakes

James Maclaine

Illustrated by Paul Parker and Becka Moor

Designed by Alice Reese

Snake consultant: Professor David Warrell,
Nuffield Department of Clinical Medicine, University of Oxford

Reading consultant: Alison Kelly

Contents

What are snakes?

Snakes are long, thin animals that have no legs.

They live in forests, mountains, deserts, grassy plains and seas.

This carpet python lives in the mountains of Australia.

There are over 3,000 different types of snakes.

Scaly skin

All snakes have skin that's dry and covered in scales.

Most snakes have smooth scales that lie flat next to each other.

You can see the smooth scales on this green cat snake's body.

Snakes shed their skin as they grow.

When a snake is ready to lose its skin, its body and eyes start to look dull.

The snake rubs its head on a rock or log, to split open the top layer of its skin.

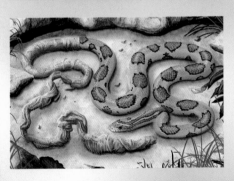

Then the snake wiggles out, leaving the old skin behind in one piece.

Spiny bush vipers aren't smooth.
They have spiky scales that stick up.

Keeping warm

Snakes are cold-blooded. This means they need the sun's heat to keep warm.

Snakes warm up their bodies by lying in the sun.

But if snakes get too hot, they have to hide from the sun.

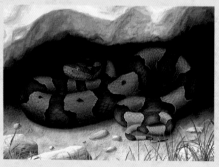

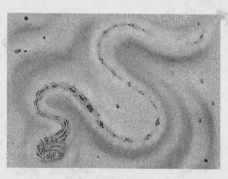

Snakes find shade under rocks...

...or bury themselves in the ground.

In winter, it is too cold for some snakes. They sleep underground. They wake up in spring when it's warm again.

These garter snakes have just woken up.

They're leaving the hole where they slept for the winter.

On the move

Snakes move around on their bellies in different ways.

Most snakes move their bodies from side to side as they slide along.

Snakes sometimes move by folding up their bodies and then stretching them out.

Large snakes often creep along in a straight line. This is a very quiet way of moving.

Some snakes move sideways over loose
sand. This is called sidewinding.

This adder is sidewinding
in the desert.

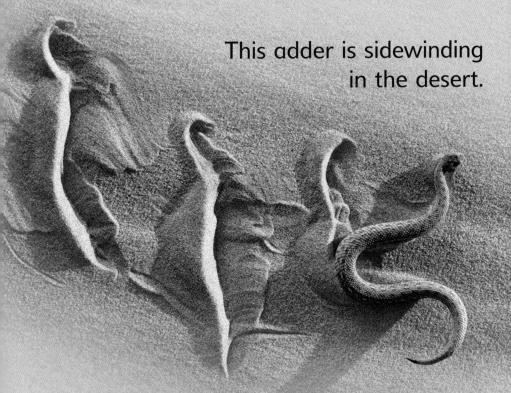

As it moves, the adder leaves a trail
in the sand.

The fastest snake is the black mamba.
It lifts up the front part of its
body as it moves.

FINISH

Up in the trees

Some snakes live in trees.
These snakes are very good
at climbing.

This snake is a
tree python.

It's gripping a branch
firmly with its scales
as it climbs.

Many snakes that
live in trees are
green. This makes
them hard to spot.

Flying snakes move from one tree to another by gliding.

The flying snake pushes itself off the end of a branch.

It bends its body and makes itself flat to help it glide through the air.

When it lands on a nearby tree, it clings on tightly.

Killer fangs

Some snakes have two long, sharp teeth called fangs.

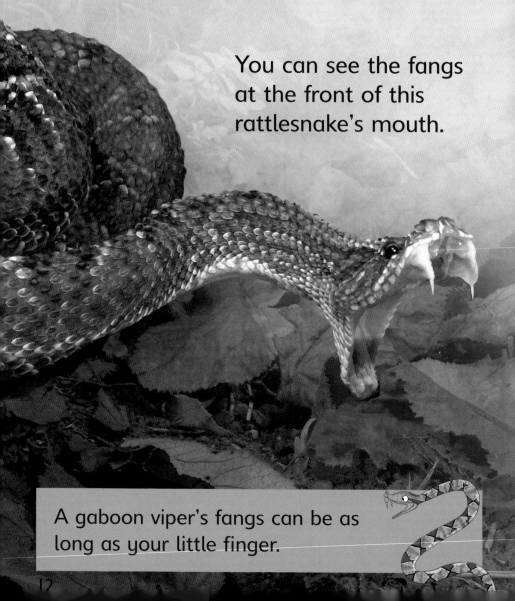

You can see the fangs at the front of this rattlesnake's mouth.

A gaboon viper's fangs can be as long as your little finger.

Snakes inject venom through their fangs to kill animals they eat.

An adder hides in some leaves and keeps very still while hunting for food.

When a lizard walks past, the adder tries to grab it quickly with its mouth.

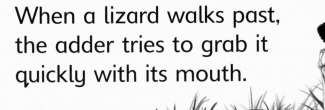

The adder bites the lizard and injects the venom. It holds on until the lizard dies.

Squeezing tight

Some snakes kill animals by squeezing them. These snakes are called constrictors.

This carpet python is squeezing a lizard with its body.

It squeezes more and more tightly until the lizard stops breathing.

Constrictors sometimes hunt very large animals, too.

A green anaconda swims along a river while hunting for deer.

Suddenly, the anaconda attacks. It grabs the deer's body with its mouth.

Then, the snake coils itself around the deer and squeezes and squeezes.

15

Big eaters

Snakes cannot chew their food so they have to swallow it whole.

A grass snake catches a frog with its mouth. Then, it starts to eat it.

The snake moves its jaws around the frog's body and swallows.

The snake keeps swallowing the frog down into its long stomach.

This snake is an egg-eater. It can eat eggs bigger than its head.

The egg's shell breaks inside the snake's throat. The snake spits the shell out.

Some snakes, such as king cobras, eat other snakes.

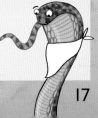

Super swimmers

All snakes can swim, but some snakes live in water.

This is a sea krait. It's a type of sea snake.

Sea snakes live in warm, tropical seas.

A sea snake swims to the surface of the water when it needs to breathe.

The snake breathes some air through its nose. Then, it dives back down.

 A yellow-bellied sea snake sheds its skin by rubbing parts of its body together.

The sea krait has a flat tail. It uses its tail like a paddle, to push through the water.

Laying eggs

Mother snakes lay long, thin eggs. The eggs have tough, leathery shells.

A mother grass snake lays her eggs in a pile of rotting plants.

The mother snake leaves the eggs as soon as she has laid them.

The plants make heat as they rot. This keeps the eggs warm.

Mother pythons and cobras take care of their eggs until they hatch.

This Indian cobra has coiled her body around her eggs to keep them warm.

Some snakes don't lay eggs. They give birth to little snakes instead.

Baby snakes

Baby snakes grow inside their eggs or their mothers' bodies for up to twelve weeks before they are born or hatch.

When a baby snake is ready to hatch, it bites a slit in the egg's shell.

Then the baby snake pushes its head out through the slit.

The snake rests. Then, it wiggles its body out of the shell.

This hog-nosed pit viper has given birth to several babies.

All baby snakes take care of themselves as soon as they are born or hatch.

Baby snakes eat insects and small animals that they catch.

Keep back!

Snakes try to scare away animals that attack them.

This rattlesnake is shaking the end of its tail to make a rattling sound.

The noise tells other animals to stay away.

Hissssss

Snakes hiss by breathing out through their noses or mouths to scare other animals.

A cobra spreads out its neck to make itself look bigger and more frightening.

A spitting cobra shoots venom from its fangs. The venom can blind an attacker.

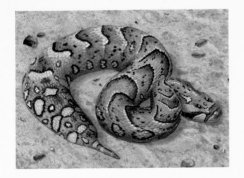

A puff adder can make its body swell up. It does this so it looks more scary.

Sneaky snakes

Some snakes use the way they look to stop animals from attacking them.

A grass snake pretends to be dead so an attacker will leave it alone.

The bright patterns on this coral snake tell other animals that it's dangerous.

A ringneck snake flashes its red belly to scare away an animal attacking it.

Other snakes use the way they look to hide while they are hunting.

A speckled rattlesnake's skin blends in with the rocks where it hunts.

A twig snake makes itself look like part of a tree to hide from animals it hunts.

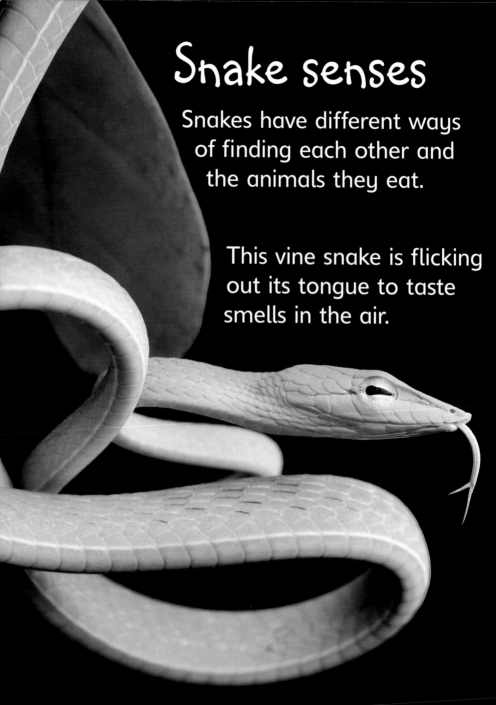

Snake senses

Snakes have different ways
of finding each other and
the animals they eat.

This vine snake is flicking
out its tongue to taste
smells in the air.

The smells tell it when an animal is nearby.

When a female snake wants to meet a male, she gives off a smell.

Some snakes find other animals by feeling the heat of their bodies. They feel heat with dimples called pits.

You can see the two pink pits on this viper's face.

Glossary

Here are some of the words in this book you might not know. This page tells you what they mean.

 scales - small parts over a snake's skin that protect its body.

 shed - to lose a layer of skin. Snakes shed their skin as they grow.

 cold-blooded - an animal that has to warm up its body in the sun.

 fangs - sharp, pointed teeth that some snakes have to inject venom.

 venom - a liquid that some snakes use to kill, stun or blind other animals.

 constrictor - a snake that squeezes animals to kill them.

 pit - a dimple on some snakes' faces. These snakes feel heat with their pits.

Websites to visit

You can visit some interesting websites to find out more about snakes.

To visit these websites, go to the Usborne Quicklinks website at **www.usborne.com/quicklinks** Read the internet safety guidelines, and then type the keywords "**beginners snakes**".

The websites are regularly reviewed and the links in Usborne Quicklinks are updated. However, Usborne Publishing is not responsible, and does not accept liability, for the content or availability of any website other than its own. We recommend that children are supervised while on the internet.

This grass snake is swimming in a pond while hunting for frogs or toads to eat.

Index

Acknowledgements

Photographic manipulation by John Russell
Cover design by Sam Chandler

Photo credits
The publishers are grateful to the following for permission to reproduce material:
cover © Michael D. Kern/naturepl.com; p1© suebg1/Getty Images; p2-3 © Michael & Patricia
Fogden/Minden Pictures/FLPA; p4 © Dorling Kindersley/Getty Images; p6 © Fabio Pupin/FLPA; p7
© Roberta Olenick/All Canada Photos/SuperStock; p9 © Solvin Zankl/naturepl.com; p10 © Thad
Samuels Abell Ii/Getty Images; p12 © Robert Pickett/Corbis; p14 © Oliver Strewe/Getty Images;
p17 © Alan J. S. Weaving/ardea.com; p18-19 © SCUBAZOO/SCIENCE PHOTO LIBRARY; p21 ©
Daniel Heuclin/NHPA/Photoshot; p23 © Michael & Patricia Fogden/Minden Pictures/FLPA; p24 ©
Joel Sartore/Getty Images; p26-27 © Fotosearch/SuperStock; p28 © Minden Pictures/SuperStock;
p29 © Michael & Patricia Fogden/Minden Pictures/FLPA; p31 © Juniors/SuperStock